Alex the kid

Talks About
Juvenile Arthritis

Alexander Draper

ISBN-13: 978-1533585448
ISBN-10: 153358544X
Printed in USA

Copyright © 2016 Alexander Draper
All rights reserved. No part of this publication may be reproduced, distributed, or transmitted in any form or by any means, including photocopying, recording, or other electronic or mechanical methods, without the prior written permission of the publisher, except in the case of brief quotations embodied in critical reviews and certain other noncommercial uses permitted by copyright law.

This book is dedicated to all of the doctors, nurses, researchers and scientists working in The Division of Rheumatology and The Division of Pediatric Rheumatology at the Hospital for Special Surgery.

A very special thanks to Thomas J.A. Lehman, MD, Chief of the Division of Pediatric Rheumatology. As one of the top doctors in your field, you care for your patients with compassion, dedication and a smile. In addition to being a superb clinician, Dr. Lehman is a rheumatology lecturer, scientist, author, fellowship mentor, world traveler and nature photographer.

Hi! My name is Alex, and I'm 7 years old. I am a normal kid.

I can play at the park with my friends.

I can swim at the beach with my little brother Max.

I can go fast on my bike.

I really like going to school to learn new things.

There is one thing I have that most other kids don't. I have Juvenile Arthritis which is often called JA or JIA.

Juvenile Arthritis makes my knee hurt, and sometimes it's hard to get out of bed in the morning.

When my knee first started hurting, my mom and dad found an awesome doctor to help me feel better. My doctor is called a rheumatologist.

He asked me some questions. Then he examined my knees and other joints too.

He sent me to get special pictures of my knees called X-rays. The X-rays didn't hurt at all.

I also had to get some lab tests.

He gave me some medicine to help my knee feel better.

Some kids with JA take medicine they swallow.

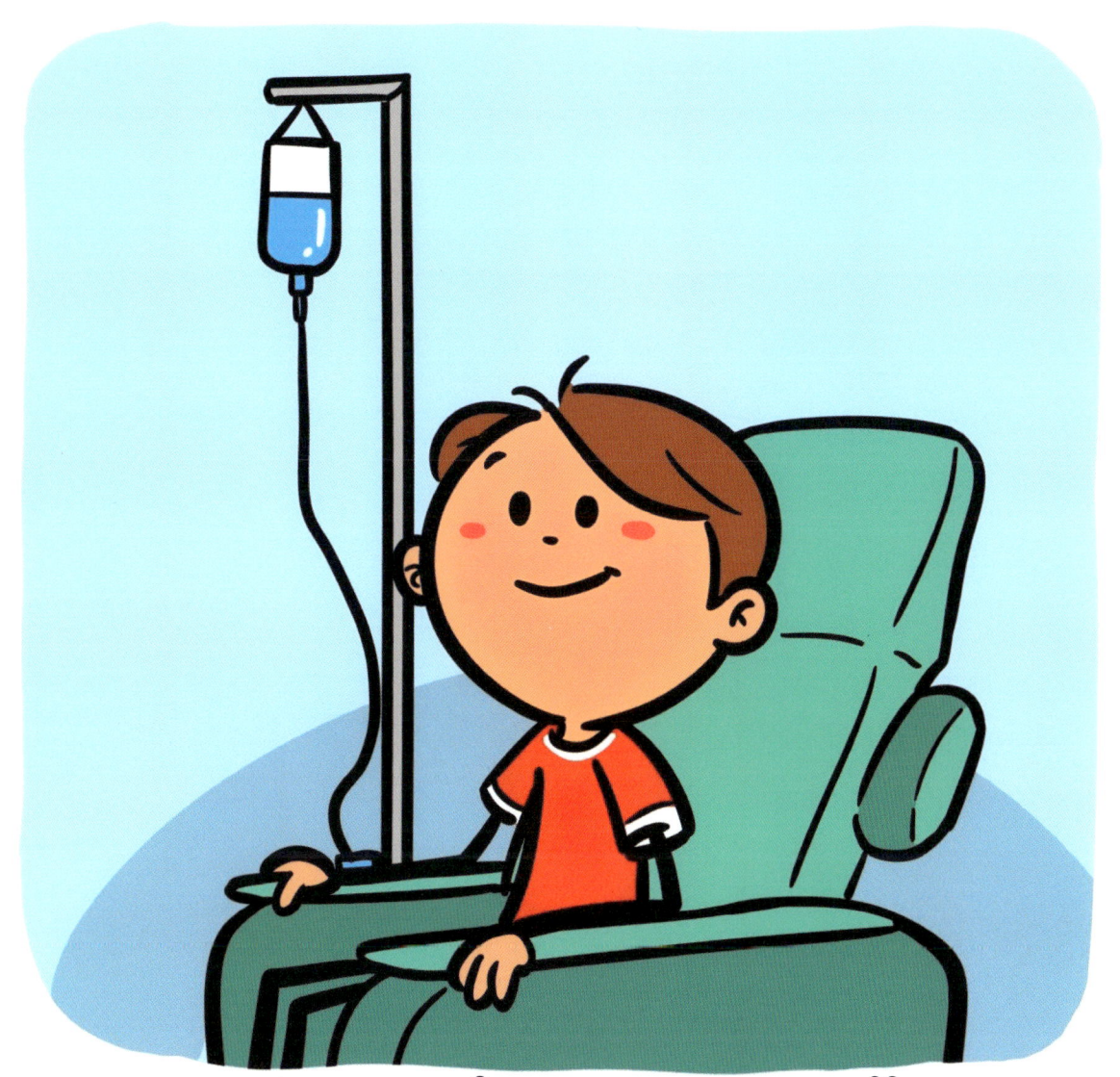

Some kids with JA get an infusion at the doctor's office or hospital.

Some kids with JA get injections.

Sometimes I get upset when I have to take my medicine, but I know it helps me to feel better.

My JA medicine is an injection that hurts for a few seconds.

But I am brave!

When I am done taking my medicine, I usually get to have an ice cream treat. Chocolate chip mint is my favorite!

Having JA is not always easy. Some days I feel mad, but everybody feels mad sometimes.

It is very important that I take good care of myself. I eat healthy foods and I keep my body active.

Playing Frisbee keeps me moving.

Jumping into a pool is lots of fun too!

I am proud to be me.

A is for Alex and JA can't stop me!

Q&A

Some Questions and Answers provided by the *National Institute of Arthritis and Musculoskeletal and Skin Diseases Juvenile Arthritis* Web Page (information on this page is not copyrighted):
http://www.niams.nih.gov/Health_Info/Juv_Arthritis/

What is Juvenile Idiopathic Arthritis?

"Arthritis" means joint inflammation. **Juvenile arthritis (JA)** is a term often used to describe arthritis in children. Children can develop almost all types of arthritis that affect adults, but the most common type that affects children is **juvenile idiopathic arthritis (JIA)**. The symptoms of juvenile idiopathic arthritis include joint pain, swelling, tenderness, warmth, and stiffness that last for more than 6 continuous weeks.

What causes Juvenile Arthritis?

Most forms of juvenile arthritis are autoimmune disorders, which means that the body's immune system—which normally helps to fight off bacteria or viruses—mistakenly attacks some of its own healthy cells and tissues. The result is inflammation, marked by redness, heat, pain, and swelling. Inflammation can cause joint damage. Doctors do not know why the immune system attacks healthy tissues in children who develop juvenile arthritis. Scientists suspect that it is a two-step process. First, something in a child's genetic makeup gives him or her a tendency to develop juvenile arthritis; then an environmental factor, such as a virus, triggers the development of the disease.

Can I catch Juvenile Arthritis like I can catch a cold or a cough?
No, Juvenile Arthritis is not contagious.

What kinds of doctors treat children with arthritis?
Sometimes children with JA are treated by pediatric rheumatologists who are doctors who have been specially trained to treat rheumatic diseases in children. However, many pediatricians and "adult" rheumatologists also treat children with juvenile arthritis. Also, all children with juvenile arthritis need to have regular exams by an ophthalmologist (eye doctor) to detect potential eye inflammation.

Do children with JA have to limit activities?
Although pain sometimes limits physical activity, exercise is important for reducing the symptoms of juvenile arthritis and maintaining function and range of motion of the joints. Most children with juvenile arthritis can

take part fully in physical activities and selected sports when their symptoms are under control. During a disease flare, however, the doctor may advise limiting certain activities, depending on the joints involved. Once the flare is over, the child can start regular activities again.

Swimming is particularly useful because it uses many joints and muscles without putting weight on the joints. A doctor or physical therapist can recommend exercises and activities.

Further reading

Some additional information on JA and JIA can be found on the following websites:

Arthritis Foundation
Website: http://www.kidsgetarthritistoo.org

Juvenile Arthritis Association
Website: http://www.juvenilearthritis.org

Hospital for Special Surgery
Website: https://www.hss.edu/conditions_juvenile-idiopathic-arthritis-overview.asp

Books about JA

- It's Not Just Growing Pains: A Guide to Childhood Muscle, Bone and Joint Pain, Rheumatic Diseases, and the Latest Treatments 1st Edition
- A Parent's Guide to Rheumatic Disease in Children

Both books are written by world renowned pediatric rheumatologist: Thomas J. A. Lehman, MD

About the Author

This is Alexander Draper's first children's book. "Alex" is currently a high school junior who is still living with JA. To keep his JA under control, Alex takes his arthritis medication and sees his doctors on a regular basis. He wrote this children's book in hopes of inspiring and encouraging other young children with JA to stay active and to feel good about themselves. In his free time, Alex enjoys going the beach, traveling with his family and repairing computers.

A portion of the proceeds of the sale of this book will be donated to various charities that support Juvenile Arthritis Research.